Love Your

Learn How to Love Who you are and Be Happy

By Sean Wells

Introduction

I want to thank you and congratulate you for downloading the book, *"Love Yourself: Learning How to Love Yourself and Be Happy"*.

This book contains proven steps and strategies on how to love yourself and be happy. This book is going to open your eyes to who you are inspite of whatever others and society have to say. The world can be such a bully and define you according to race, ethnicity, class, economic status, intelligence, popularity etc. It has set many standards and niches which it wants to bucket you in and that is making you miserable and unsuccessful.

Not anymore.

This book promises to teach you how to learn to love yourself by finding and accepting it. And by finding and accepting, this book doesn't just mean past experiences, personal history or parental lineage. This book will teach you that the first step to loving who you are is accepting what you chose to be despite whatever society says you are. Finding, choosing and accepting who you want to be will help you love and be happy with who you are. It will determine what future has in store for you and it will help you go through life and adversity with a firm purpose and resolve.

Thanks again for downloading this book. I hope you enjoy it!

Why I Wrote This Book

I wrote this book for the following reasons:

1. There is so much more to life than the daily dreary drudgery of existence. All you need to do is learn to love yourself and let that love give you hope, assurance and happiness.

2. Society may have already classified and bucketed you as a loser, or an undesirable because of your past deeds, mistakes and choices. However, that is no reason to remain unloved even by yourself. Learn to love yourself and look beyond the labels and judgments. Discover self-respect and discover the uniqueness in you.

3. You may believe you are unlovable for whatever your reason but you're not. Just because you think that no one loves you doesn't mean you shouldn't love yourself too. Learn to love yourself and let that love pull you out of the pit of undesirability and rejection. Let it endow you with self-esteem and make you see the value that lies hidden in you.

Why You Should Read This Book

This book will help you learn to love who you are and be happy.

Have you ever asked yourself the following?

Do you refuse to accept what society has bucketed you?

Are you having difficulty believing and accepting that your past experience, your parental lineage or your personal history has destined you to be what you are now?

Are you are like many people who go through life believing that fate has you stuck on an inescapable road that leads to failure and unhappiness?

Have you been dealt a bad hand too many times to think that winning the game of life is an impossibility and a better life is not a choice?

Are you like many who once relied on others and clung to God, a spouse, friends, parents and family for that comforting love and happiness and suddenly find yourself deprived because of life's adversities?

Is the highway that we call life so littered with speed bumps, slick curves and troublesome spots that keep derailing your pursuit of happiness?

Has death, career loss or divorce left you so unsure, insecure and disappointed with yourself?

Finally, have you given up on ever experiencing love and happiness?

If life has you plagued with the aforementioned questions, read this book.

Copyright

Disclaimer

The information provided in this book is designed to provide helpful information on the subjects discussed. This book is not meant to be used, nor should it be used, to diagnose or treat any medical condition. For diagnosis or treatment of any medical problem, consult your own physician. The publisher and author are not responsible for any specific health or allergy needs that may require medical supervision and are not liable for any damages or negative consequences from any treatment, action, application or preparation, to any person reading or following the information in this book. Any references included are provided for informational purposes only and do not constitute endorsement of any websites or other sources. Readers should be aware that any websites listed in this book may change.

Table of Contents

What Does It Mean To Love Yourself

Mention loving yourself to someone and you would get three opinions. The first opinion would most likely be that you're conceited. The second is that you're an egoist and a narcissist. The third which is more likely to come from those who really know you the most, is that is wonderful.

Conceit

Conceit as defined is an over-inflated sense of self-esteem or self-worth. Self-esteem or being cognizant of and respecting one's abilities, achievements and value is a good thing. When all that gets into your head and you start become too proud and arrogant then it becomes conceit.

Here is a little quiz to find out if you are conceited or genuinely love yourself:

1. You achievements and successes are proof of how extraordinary you are.

2. You disdain the company of people whose achievements and successes do not equal yours

3. You belittle the achievements and successes of others and you feel threatened when they appear to surpass you.

4. You pin the blame on anyone for any failures or disappointments.

5. You demand that respect and honor.

If you find yourself arguing with each point in the quiz and excusing or denying that any of it pertains to you, you may have a little challenge to overcome. And that's putting it politely.

Egotism and Narcissism

The world hates egotists and narcissists. It absolutely abhors anyone who think the sun shines out of his behind or the world revolves around her little finger. Society reserves viral posts and sleazy gossip columns for those whose favorite pronouns are I, me and my. On the other hand, it holds out its contempt for those individuals who are so enamored with themselves and who think they are the embodiment of perfection. Hollywood, Bollywood and the paparazzi may throw out a pedestal, a runway or a stage for these but by and large, the world is scandalized that both have no other care or concern except for adulation and pedestals to stand on.

Conceit, egotism and narcissism all have a common element that isn't love: vanity. So is loving oneself just another display of vanity or is it something else?

Let's look at an example of selflessness and see if it approaches a genuine love for oneself:

Martyrdom

The world loves martyrs. It praises those who willingly give up everything even their own identities for others. It salutes those who willingly sacrifice even life if necessary for the greater good. It honors the likes of Mandela, Gandhi and Pope Francis 1. To many, martyrdom is the ultimate example of selfless love.

Is it?

Some psychologists believe that martyrdom while appearing to be good, is just another expression of megalomania and that many self-proclaimed martyrs are inwardly egotists and conceited beings. Under the mantel of selflessness and a professed kindness for others lurks a sinister motive that is driven by the desire to be a "living" saint or a modern-day hero. An examination of many famous last words including those about to die for a cause have indicated a motivation for their place in history to be secured or to be honored with a coveted place near the throne of God.

Simply put, martyrdom is just another extreme form of humble brag: a Justin Bieber going around town doing deeds worthy of Mother Teresa and bragging about it on Twitter.

St Paul offers the best insights into what it means to love yourself.

Really Loving Yourself

In the 13th Chapter of his first letter to the Corinthians, St Paul offers a criterion which we could use to discern between really love yourself and not just being conceited, egotistic or narcissistic. His discourse draws a line between the genuine love and the hollowness of the other three which he described as "sounding brass or tinkling cymbals." These qualities of real self-love are as follows:

Long Suffering and Kind

It's easy to be patient or long suffering with the tantrums of kids, the whines of friends or the uncouth behavior of strangers, bosses and colleagues. It is also not difficult to be kind to strangers. However, when it comes to yourself, you are either too impatient or too frustrated with your efforts. You can also be too harsh and demanding often expecting too much or holding yourself up to a standard higher than you extend to others. That is already beyond self-martyrdom and can be very demotivating.

To really love yourself means giving yourself the same latitude to grow and learn from your mistakes that you made that has affected others. It also means being kind to yourself first, understanding your own weaknesses and not judging yourself too harshly. It doesn't mean constantly asking "what's in it for me" but giving yourself a pat on the back for a job well done, giving time for yourself to learn and develop and acknowledging you can't be Superman 24/7.

Not Puffed Up and Does Not Parade Itself

To those who think that loving yourself means being egoistic, St Paul has these to say: don't be puffed up and don't parade.

To understand what being puffed up and parading your love means, you need only to look at Hollywood, TMZ and the tabloids and see what all those stars are doing to grab the limelight and attention. It's even more irritating to see the same kind of vanity and false sense of entitlement in other people.

Loving yourself doesn't mean you can't focus on your needs, desires and aspirations or appreciate and acknowledge your gifts, skills and talents. Flaunting it in the faces of others and making the world acknowledge your vanity is actually more of a symptom of insecurity rather love, and so is always needing a runway or a stage to strut and parade on. You certainly do not need either if you truly love yourself.

Thinks no evil

Perhaps the best characteristics of truly loving oneself is not being able to think evil about who you are. This does not mean denial of any flaw, imperfection or lack of talent. Rather thinking no evil means not debasing yourself to the point of losing all self-esteem and self-respect.

When you think of yourself as too dumb or stupid to change for the better, that is thinking evil of yourself. It is the same when you think it is your fate and destiny to be stuck in a quagmire just because you have been there for so long. Thinking evil and not loving yourself is when you find fault with every adverse incident in your life has if the universe conspired against you.

Rejoices in the truth

Rejoicing in the truth simply means acknowledging what you are AND what you can become. Acknowledging weaknesses, strengths, positive traits and opportunities to improve on is a trademark of truly loving yourself. The resentment of anything other than adulation, the denial of any wrong, and the resentment at any insinuation of infallibility is a trademark of narcissism, conceit and vanity but not a genuine love for one's self.

Believes, Hopes and Endures

Anyone who continues to believe and hope in himself amidst adversity and circumstances and willingly bears and endures all things truly loves himself or herself. A person who gives up in frustration and finds no hope at all is someone who is just about to give up on loving himself. A person who has lost self-respect, personal dignity and no longer believes in himself, cannot genuinely say he or she loves himself.

There is so much more in the apostle's epistle that identify what it means to love yourself but these should be sufficient to indicate whether you are just wallowing in vanity or genuinely need to learn to love yourself. If it does, then read on.

Know Who You Are

In order to learn to love yourself and be happy, there are three important steps to accomplish. These are:

1. Know who you are

2. Accept who you are

3. Know what you can become

Let's discuss the first step:

Know Who You Are

What does it mean to know who you are?

Knowing who you are means more than just knowing your name, biographical information, parental lineage or ancestry or genetic history. Knowing who you are means finding out your identify and purpose. Many a socialite has shocked the world by being so miserable inspite of lavish comfort and possession of every desirable gadget or artifact. These poor souls drown themselves in alcohol, illicit drugs or sex to find meaning for their existence. Others ascend to ascetism or go into extreme forms of religion to find that purpose. And there are others who find no comfort except from an overdose, a slashed wrist or a bullet to the forehead.

Here are three statements to help you find out who you are and begin learning to love yourself.

You are Unique

That is correct. Out of the 7 billion persons living on the planet today, there is no one like you. There maybe those who share the same skin color, genes or behavior but there is no one who is an exact duplicate of who you are.

What does that mean?

Simply, that you have talents, abilities, dreams, challenges and nuggets of wisdom that no one else has not even in your own family. The absence of limbs, abilities or opportunities does not diminish your uniqueness but enhances it.

That said, because you are unique, you are the piece of the puzzle without which the picture of humanity will never be completed.

You are valuable

That may be difficult to believe but until you reach the end of the road called life, you will never know. The value that you possess is not in how much cash you have in your wallet or in the bank. It is not measured by the extent of your holdings or by the breadth of power that you possess. It may not even be in the sphere of influence that you have over those around you.

Your value is like that of a diamond encased in rock. Just because, the miners have not dug it out of the mineshaft or freed it from its rocky prison does not mean that the diamond is not valuable. Just because you are alone and perhaps useless in the sight of many does not that you are insignificant, of no worth and useless. Remember, a single iota may be insignificant but its absence denies perfection.

You are Not What Others Think you are

Psychologists have made the observation in some children who are denied any positive reinforcement and who are constantly told that they are bad after every mistake. While many grew up with this mindset, there have been a few who resisted the brainwash and did not fall into the same lifestyle as others. Man may be affected by his environment and be influenced by the pressures around him but part of his uniqueness allows him to break free from the mold of conformity if given the chance.

As poignantly illustrated in the cult classic, *Gattaca*, there is no gene for the human spirit. There will always be someone who will go against the flow and who will break free of the herd and choose his own destiny.

This simply means that in spite of the long history of generations before you, you are not what others say you are. There is no fate or destiny other than what you hold in your hands. Others may chain you, brand you, make you conform to their will and remake you into their own image, but only if you allow them to do so.

You are a Child of the Universe

There are those who found comfort in identifying themselves as members of the master race. Others cling to the idea that they are the evolved descendants of a long chain of human progression through millennia. Others identify themselves as children of God.

Whatever it is, there is one thing for certain. Out of a million, billion trillion possibilities and creations, you are the only one who is exactly like you. And you stand among 7 billion humans in a world that is but one among a billion possible worlds among a million possible galaxies in an infinitely expanding universe. Others may find that insignificant but the fact remains that there is only one you: the single piece that without which the universe can never be made perfect.

Accept Who You Are

Acceptance is a double-edged sword.

On one hand is to accept what your current situation is as fate and live and perish according to what it dictates. On the other hand is to accept your uniqueness and value and break free.

When learning to love yourself, the acceptance of fate or karma is to speak evil and to deny yourself of hope. It is not genuinely loving yourself to say, "I accept my fate. I surrender to my karma." Once you do you are giving in to the vanity of martyrdom and the stubbornness of pride that exists only in a narcissist or an egotist.

Here are the things you should learn to accept without resigning yourself:

Acknowledge your Weaknesses

No man is perfect but many deny their imperfections and refuse to acknowledge their mistakes and failures. That is not really loving yourself if you do.

You must learn to recognize that there are things beyond your control which limit your opportunities or abilities. That is not to say that you surrender yourself, but like a brilliant tactician, that is to acknowledge what you need to fortify, build up or strengthen. For instance, an alcoholic who recognizes that his fondness for the company of his company at the bar is what keeps provoking his addiction, knows that he will need to remove himself from such environment if he is to be cured. On the other hand, the alcoholic who says he needs the comfort of the bar and his friends, will never succeed in breaking his craving for alcohol.

Part of knowing who you are is owning up to your weaknesses, your failures and your inabilities.

Recognize Your Strengths

Just as everyone has weaknesses, so does everyone has strengths. That is part of your uniqueness. Society may have discovered that and now seeks to destroy it by influencing you to believe that you don't. Part of knowing who you are is knowing what your strengths are. Part of loving yourself is embracing those strengths and making them a part of you despite whatever society says. Look to Beethoven, a deaf musician who composed many of the world's classic masterpieces. Or Handel, starving and impoverished when he wrote his famous oratorio *The Messiah*. J. K. Rawlings was destitute on a train when she came up with what became a 7 volume bestseller and a string of box office hits. Alexander Graham Bell may not be recognized in the field of speech pathology where he first started, but the whole world knows him as the inventor of the telephone.

Your strengths may not be what society sees or accepts but they are strengths nonetheless and your task is to build them up if you are to really learn to love yourself.

Value your Identity

Today's world is full of copycats and idol worshippers. Everyone aspires to become the next Beyoncé, the future Obama or the new Oprah. No one seems to want to be themselves these days as Bon Jovi sang about. And if that isn't worse, there are those who do not even want to be anybody and just be someone lost in crowd or another cog in the mass of humanity.

That is wrong.

If you are to learn to love yourself you must learn to value who you are, your uniqueness and your identity. You must learn to value your being a person even if society spits on you and tramples you down.

Accept Choice and Accountability

The final step to accept the responsibility of making a choice and the accountability that accompanies it. This is the most difficult especially for anyone who has known nothing but depravity, disappointment or rejection since birth. It is also very difficult in the acknowledgement of weaknesses, one discovers the consequences of poor choices made. Yet these are the most important proofs of genuinely loving yourself. You cannot claim to really love yourself after identifying and accepting who you are, if you are not willing to make a choice to break free or accept accountability for that choice. The choice you make to resign yourself to fate or karma is tantamount to surrendering your love for yourself and with it your dignity, self-esteem, self-respect and self-worth. That is also the same when you try to escape or excuse your responsibility for the consequence of past choices. On the other hand, the choice to become who you really are and to accept the accountability for whatever you decide to do, will strengthen your will, confidence and spirit. It will allow you to speak no evil of yourself, to rejoice in who you are, to hope and believe, and then to bear and endure with long suffering. You may not be able to break free from circumstance but you will have really learned to love yourself and achieve a measure of happiness.

Have you accepted that choice?

Achieve What You Can Become

So you have completed the first two steps to learning to love yourself. You discovered and known who you are. You have accepted your weaknesses, strengths and value. You have made a choice to become who you really are.

Here are a few steps to achieve who you can become:

Make a Goal

Making a goal is like charting a course to one's destination. It is one thing to know you need to get to New York. It is another thing to plan the trip to New York. Lying around the house and dreaming about getting to New York and what you will do when you get there is not going to get you any closer to that goal. You need to figure how much the trip would cost, how much you need to save, what you need to do to prepare and then start working on it. Remember a journey is not one massive leap across the sky but a series of steps that you need to make a few at a time. You can try practicing how to make giant leaps but unless the cosmos endows you with great power, you might want to start making those steps.

Believe That You Can Achieve

The next step once you have made a goal to achieve what you can become, is to believe. That will further ignite the sparks of truly loving yourself and fan them into a flame that will give you self-confidence and self-assurance.

Believing that you can achieve is not something difficult when you break down your goal into something manageable and when you continue to persevere with hope and patience.

Take Baby Steps

This goes back to making a goal and believing you can achieve it. Learning how to make giant bounds is not impossible: you just don't have someone to teach you how to do it and doing it yourself might take a long time. However, remember when you were a toddler learning how to walk? Take that principle and apply it to your goal by breaking it down into manageable steps or goals which you can measure and which will continue to build your confidence.

Going back to example of going to New York, your baby steps would probably be saving for a bus ticket and that can even be broken down into saving a few dollars each day until you have enough for a ticket to the Big Apple.

Keep at it

A baby who takes a few steps then reverts to crawling will never learn to walk unless it keeps standing up and taking a few more steps. Similarly, you'll never achieve your goal if you suddenly stop or quit after a few setbacks. Remember there is never a smooth road in life so expect to stumble, fall or slide back. But keep at it even if you have to slowdown. The key is never to lose sight of the goal. Take a lesson from Abraham Lincoln who never lost sight of his political vision and kept running inspite of several political setbacks and losses.

Don't Give Up

On your journey to achieve what you can become, life throws you more than a puddle and crashes a huge or insurmountable roadblock. Such was the case with Handel who suddenly fell out of favor, sunk into debt and got totally impoverished before he wrote *The Messiah*. The same is true with Thomas Edison whose invention after invention caught some attention but never the big break he was looking for until he invented the incandescent lamp.

The road to hell is littered with lofty goals left unaccomplished because those who made them gave up and gave in to fate and karma. Gandhi would have been a successful lawyer in England or South Africa if he gave up his dream but he wouldn't have fathered the independent republic of India. Mandela would have languished in prison or retired to a quiet life after it but a non-apartheid South Africa would not have come into being.

Never give up on a goal. Rest if you must. Work on a different path if necessary but do not give up on achieving what you can become. Keep believing. Keep hoping and keep enduring. The result will be finally learning to love yourself and becoming happy.

Love Yourself

Whether or not you have achieved what you seek out to become or are still working on the goals, the seeds of genuine love for yourself would have already been planted. You would have already discovered so many reasons not to hate yourself. You would have embraced an identity as a child of God and not just a random creature spawned by some chemical reaction. You might have uncovered talents and abilities that you never knew you had. You would identified and overcome certain character flaws and weaknesses.

Here are some signs that you have genuinely begun to love yourself:

Self-confidence

Self-confidence is a feeling of assurance in one's abilities to become successful and accomplish something. Even if the outcome is a failure, if the feeling persist that you can do better the next time, that still indicates self-confidence.

Self-confidence is present when you no longer feel the need to compare yourself to others. It doing so brings out a feeling of superiority, then that is vanity and the beginning of conceit, egotism or narcissism. On the other hand, if the comparison results into a feeling of inferiority, this means a loss of self-confidence or a lack of self-worth.

Self-confidence grows when you accept yourself as a unique individual with no need to compare yourself to others.

Self-respect

Self-respect is knowing you are a unique individual with a distinct personality, traits and abilities and not just a cog in the mass of humanity. It is being able to look up to yourself with dignity and to reverence your body.

Most people who have lost a sense of self-respect too often do not care if their behavior offends, if their attire is tatters or if drugs and substances are weakening their bodies. On the other hand, one who possesses self-respect will make sure to care for his or her health and even diet or exercise. He or she will dress appropriately in order to attract the same level of respect from others rather than dress down to look like a piece of meat. He or she will get out of addiction and will strive to be as dignified as possible.

Even in the most destitute of circumstance, a person with self-respect will do his or her utmost best to be independent, polite, self-reliant or dignified. It is neither clothes, possessions, a car, home nor a job that gives you self-respect. It is the demeanor and the attitude that shows from under the grime and stress of daily living.

Self-esteem

Self-esteem is how you show how much you value yourself. It can be manifested by a show of self-confidence or by a dislike or even disgust in your situation, behavior or your current status. How you face adversity is often the litmus test of your self-esteem. If you are frustrated or depressed that often shows a lack of self-esteem unlike when you are hopeful, enduring and patient.

If you do not love really yourself, you usually try to make others love you by lowering your personal values and morals. The boundaries you set for yourself are often an indication of how much you value or esteem yourself to be. When you use all means necessary to protect your life, keep yourself healthy and avoid falling into bad company, that displays how much self-esteem you have and with it how much you have learned to love yourself.

Self-forgiveness

A sure sign that you have learned to love yourself is when you have accepted your faults, made amends and forgiven yourself. Acknowledging past errors is one thing. Forgiving yourself for having caused them is another. When regrets and the memories of past deeds continue to haunt your mind even after all the repentance and restitution given, you need to let go and give yourself a break from the past. Otherwise, it will continue to become a barrier against learning how to love and be happy.

Adding these to the attributes identified by St Paul, should give you an indication of how much you have learned to love yourself.

Now all you need is to be happy.

Be Happy

Being happy is the natural outcome of having learned to love yourself. Knowing that you have great value and that you are striving to become what you should be doesn't mean you have to be so glum and stoic. In fact, if after all you do to learn to love yourself and still not feel happy is an indication of something you are either holding back, unwilling to accept or refusing to do.

Here are two signs of happiness that come from genuinely loving yourself:

Self-assurance

If self-confidence is trusting in your abilities, talents, strength and capabilities, self-assurance is knowing what you are doing is the right thing to do and where you are headed is the right place to go. It means not being worried that you might have made the wrong choice or being frustrated by the adversities and the obstacles you encounter.

Self-assurance is what gives you the hope to keep going and the endurance and patience to not want to give up.

Peace of Mind

Happiness is more a state of peace than peals of maniacal laughter. When your mind is no longer haunted by past sins, mistakes and failures, you are inwardly happy. When you are able to look people even former friends or current enemies squarely in the eye without a twitch of guilt or even fear, which is a hallmark of happiness.

Peace of mind comes knowing that you have accepted your faults and weaknesses and have rendered your *mea culpa*. It comes when you have completed making amends

The Greatest Love of All

At this point, you are probably feeling good about yourself. You feel self-assured and have peace of mind. You are oozing with self-confidence, self-respect and self-esteem. You could say you have learned to love yourself and become truly happy.

Yet are you?

There is a fine line behind what you feel from that of a narcissist, egotist and a conceited fool.

The line is in love itself.

Going back to St Paul's discourse on love to the Corinthians, he mentioned love as nothing but air blowing through brass instruments without the attributes of love being applied to love others including being kind, long suffering, hoping, bearing, believing and enduring, thinking no evil and rejoicing in the truth.

Christ clarified that further when He mentioned the second greatest commandment to love others as you love yourself and to love your enemies. And as if that were not enough, He spoke about laying down one's life for a friend as a love no greater than any and then proceeded to make Himself an example.

Finding the greatest love by learning to love yourself doesn't become more significant and more substantive until you extend that love to others. As someone anonymous once said, "Your love for yourself is not made full until you shine it like a mirror on others."

Do so and you will have finally learned to love yourself and become happy.

Bonus Chapter – Overcoming Adversity

Adversity is often what makes or breaks any attempt to learn to love yourself and be happy. Depending on its severity, it can totally trash any progress you made and turn you into something cynical, disbelieving or depressed.

However that need not be the case. Oftentimes, when viewed from the lens of hindsight, adversity turns out to be a learning experience or a pivotal point from which you could have emerged happy and self-assured had you acted differently.

Unfortunately, hindsight always comes last. However, that does not mean that you are unable to overcome adversity.

Here are a few tips to remember so that adversity does not derail you from learning to love yourself:

Adversity is Not a Curse

Oftentimes, when we view things as a curse or a spell of doom or fate upon us, we become cynical and disbelieving. However, no one looks as a cycle that way or a hurricane or a typhoon. When viewed as natural phenomena, people who do are generally able to pick themselves up and rebuild. By the same token, tribal communities who believed a storm was caused by a witch turn into a mob and descend into a frenzy that resolves none of the storm's damages.

The same is true with adversity. View it as a fact of life and move on no matter how painful. View it as your fault or somebody else and all you will get is an endless blame game that will bring nothing good in return.

Move On

When a storm ravages a seaside village, the villagers either rebuild or move further inland. When a fire decimates a crop, the farmer either replants what he is able or works elsewhere while waiting to recover. In like manner, when adversity comes, pick up what it leaves you and move on. You can mourn and cry over the ashes as long and as appropriate but the best way to overcome adversity is to move on.

Let it Blow Over

When adversity comes, oftentimes the best way to get over it is to let it blow over like a storm. There is no sense fighting a hurricane. Instead hunker down and let the comforting arms of love shelter you.

Conclusion

At the end of the day, whether you learn to love yourself and be happy is all up to you. It is after all a matter of choice and not a matter of fate. Maybe, circumstance or adversity put you where you are right now. Perhaps what you have is a result of an accumulation of choices and mistakes.

Whatever it is that brought you to where you are does not matter as much as where you are to go from here. If society has judged you, you can just lay back down and accept it. Or you can set sights on a new tomorrow and start afresh.

There is nothing to bar you from accepting defeat and surrendering you peace of mind, self-assurance or self-competence. Many find that a convenient excuse to just go with the flow or even end life.

However, for those who decided to learn to love themselves, life springs back like spring after a cold dreary winter. Happiness is reborn and enthusiasm for life occurs and the darkness of the past is overshadowed by the hope of tomorrow.

Do you want to be happy?

Do you want to be loved?

Do you want the assurance, esteem, respect and confidence from loving yourself?

The choice is up to you.

May this book provide you the inspiration to take the next steps forward and achieve whatever it is your heart desires.

Thank you again and a safe journey through life.

One Last Thing...

If you enjoyed this book or found it useful I'd be very grateful if you'd post a short review on Amazon. Your support really does make a difference and I read all the reviews personally so I can get your feedback and make this book even better.

If you'd like to leave a review then all you need to do is click the review link on this book's page...

Thank You so Much

31383916R00016

Printed in Poland
by Amazon Fulfillment
Poland Sp. z o.o., Wrocław